ST

QUESTIONS FOR

THE HIDDEN

WORDS OF

BAHÁ'U'LLÁH

by
Jan Perry

www.SereneWomen.com

ISBN-13:978-1537590509

ISBN-10:1537590502

Book Layout ©2017 BookDesignTemplates.com

Ordering Information:
Quantity sales. Special discounts are available on quantity purchases by corporations, associations, and others. For details, contact the "Special Sales Department" at the address above.

Study Questions for The Hidden Words of Bahá'u'lláh / Jan Perry. -- 1st ed.
ISBN-13:978-1537590509

Forward

Why was this book assembled?

Recite ye the verses of God every morn and eventide. Whoso faileth to recite them hath not been faithful to the Covenant of God and His Testament, and whoso turneth away from these holy verses in this Day is of those who throughout eternity have turned away from God. Fear ye God, O My servants, one and all. Pride not yourselves on much reading of the verses or on a multitude of pious acts by night and day; for were a man to read a single verse with joy and radiance it would be better for him than to read with lassitude all the Holy Books of God, the Help in Peril, the Self-Subsisting. Read ye the sacred verses in such measure that ye be not overcome by languor and de-spondency. Lay not upon your souls that which will weary them and weigh them down, but rather what will lighten and uplift them, so that they may soar on the wings of the Divine verses towards the Dawning-place of His manifest signs; this will draw you nearer to God, did ye but comprehend.

Bahá'u'lláh: Kitáb-i-Aqdas, p. 73-74

They who recite the verses of the All-Merciful in the most me-lodious of tones will perceive in them that with which the sov-ereignty of earth and heaven can never be compared. From them they will inhale the divine fragrance of My worlds – worlds which today none can discern save those who have been endowed with vision through this sublime, this beauteous Revelation. Say: These verses draw hearts that are pure unto those spiritual worlds that can neither be expressed in words nor intimated by allusion. Blessed be those who hearken.

Bahá'u'lláh: Kitáb-i-Aqdas, p. 61

Nevertheless some thoughts are useless to man; they are like waves moving in the sea without result. But if the faculty of meditation is bathed in the inner light and characterized with divine attributes, the results will be confirmed.

The meditative faculty is akin to the mirror; if you put it before earthly objects it will reflect them. Therefore if the spirit of man is contemplating earthly subjects he will be informed of these.

But if you turn the mirror of your spirits heavenwards, the heavenly constellations and the rays of the Sun of Reality will be reflected in your hearts, and the virtues of the Kingdom will be obtained.

Therefore let us keep this faculty rightly directed - turning it to the heavenly Sun and not to earthly objects - so that we may discover the secrets of the Kingdom, and comprehend the allegories of the Bible and the mysteries of the spirit.

'Abdu'l-Bahá, Paris Talks, pp. 175-176

Why questions?

...an understanding of the Writings must begin by focusing the mind on what is being read before allowing one's imagination to roam and personal opinions to flow freely. It is quite likely that by first developing in the believers, early in their study of the Faith, a capacity to focus attention on the immediate and explicit meaning of sentences they read from the Holy Writings, we will be contributing to the creation of unity of thought in our communities, since such a unity can only be attained when personal opinions are illuminated by Divine Wisdom.

Ruhi Institute, Book 1, Reflections on the life of the Spirit, p. 1

How to use this book

With a copy of *The Hidden* Words beside this book, read the indicated Hidden Word and reflect on the questions that are meaningful to you. Think about how the Hidden Word applies to you and your life. White space is available for you to jot down your thoughts.

THE HIDDEN WORDS OF BAHÁ'U'LLÁH

Part I – from the Arabic

HIDDEN WORDS INTRODUCTORY COMMENTS

QUESTIONS

Where have these words come from?

Why has God revealed the Hidden Words for us?

What are we to fulfill in our lives?

QUESTIONS

What do we need to do to have an ancient, imperishable, and everlasting sovereignty?

What happens if we possess a pure, kindly and radiant heart?

What kind of sovereignty could be ours?

How can I apply this in my life today?

QUESTIONS

What do we need to do if we want God to confide in us?

How will justice let us see, hear, and know?

What is the best beloved thing in the sight of God?

How can I apply this in my life today?

QUESTIONS

Why did God create us?

Why has God revealed His beauty to us?

Where did God know his love for us?

What did God engrave on us?

How can I apply this in my life today?

QUESTIONS

What do we need to do so that God may fill our souls with the spirit of life?

Why were we created?

What does it mean for God to name our name?

How can I apply this in my life today?

Questions

Why should we love God?

What happens if we do not love Him?

What should we know?

What does it mean for us to be referred to as "O Son Of Being?"

How can I apply this in my life today?

QUESTIONS

What is our heavenly home?

What is our Paradise?

What has been destined for us?

How can I apply this in my life today?

QUESTION

If we love God, what should we do?

Why should we not regard our own pleasure?

What do we need to do so that God can eternally live within us?

How can I apply this in my life today?

QUESTIONS

How does God desire to be loved?

Where is our peace?

How do we glory in God's name?

How can I apply this in my life today?

QUESTIONS

What is God's stronghold?

Where are we safe and secure?

What happens if we turn away from God's love?

How can I apply this in my life today?

QUESTIONS

Where can we abide in safety?

What is God's stronghold?

Where is God's love?

How can I apply this in my life today?

QUESTIONS

What are we to get our radiance?

Where is God's light?

What has God shed upon us?

How has God created us?

How can I apply this in my life today?

QUESTIONS

How did God create us?

What are we to be content with?

What are we not to doubt?

Where has God placed his light?

How can I apply this in my life today?

ARABIC HIDDEN WORDS #13

QUESTIONS

How did God create us?

What do we do to ourselves?

Where is God Standing?

What is within us?

How can I apply this in my life today?

QUESTIONS

How does God describe us?

What do we fear?

Where should we abide to find God in the realm of glory?

How can I apply this in my life today?

QUESTIONS

Where should we turn our face?

If we seek someone other than God, how will our quest end?

What does it mean to be addressed as "O Son of Utterance?"

How can I apply this in my life today?

QUESTIONS

Who are we to commune with?

What is the essence of God's command?

What does it mean to be the Son of Light?

How can I apply this in my life today?

ARABIC HIDDEN WORDS #17

QUESTIONS

What are we to be content with?

What is the only thing that can suffice us?

What does it look like when we are content with God?

How can I apply this in my life today?

Questions

What are we to be content with?

What is the condition that we must meet to benefit from what God has ordained for us?

What should we not ask God for?

How can I apply this in my life today?

QUESTIONS

What has been breathed into us?

Why was it breathed into us?

Why would God address us as Son of Wondrous Vision?

How can I apply this in my life today?

QUESTIONS

What cannot be forgotten?

How can we describe God's grace to us?

What is manifest in us?

How might we obscure God's light that is within us?

How can I apply this in my life today?

QUESTIONS

What has God given us?
What are we to return to?
What are the choicest fruits?
How can I apply this in my life today?

QUESTIONS

How did God create us?

What are we to rise to?

What have we done to ourselves?

What were we created for?

How can I apply this in my life today?

QUESTIONS

What does God call us to?

What do we seek?

What makes us turn away from God and toward our own desires?

How can I apply this in my life today?

QUESTIONS

What are we not to transgress?

What are we not to claim?

Where should we prostrate ourselves?

What are our limits and what does not beseem us?

How can I apply this in my life today?

Questions

Who leads the poor in their way?

Who should we not vaunt ourselves over?

How does God behold us?

How can I apply this in my life today?

QUESTIONS

How does God address us?

Who is accursed of God?

What does it mean to be a Son Of Being?

What are we doing when we busy ourselves with the faults of others?

How can I apply this in my life today?

Questions

If we have sinned, what should we not do?

If we talk about the sins of others, what happens to us?

How do we avoid talking about the sins of others?

How can I apply this in my life today?

QUESTIONS

Who is not of God?

If one does not bid others to be just, is it OK to commit iniquity?

Does calling ourselves Bahá'is mean that we are Bahá'is?

How can I apply this in my life today?

QUESTIONS

What should we not ascribe to anyone else?

What should we not say?

What does it mean to say not that which thou doest not?

How can I apply this in my life today?

QUESTIONS

What should we deny God's servants?

Whose face does one of God's servants represent?

How can I apply this in my life today?

QUESTIONS

What should we do each day?

What will we be asked to do when death comes upon us?

How do we bring ourselves to account?

How can I apply this in my life today?

QUESTIONS

What is death?

What is to shed its splendor upon us?

How do we veil ourselves from the light?

How can I apply this in my life today?

QUESTIONS:

How does God hail us?

To live in peace for evermore, where should we abide?

How do we abide in the court of holiness?

How can I apply this in my life today?

QUESTIONS

What does the spirit of holiness bring us?

What leads us?

What confirms us?

What is the spirit of power?

How can I apply this in my life today?

QUESTIONS

What is the reason that we should sorrow?
What is the reason that we should rejoice?
What can we do to draw nearer to God?
How can I apply this in my life today?

QUESTIONS

What do we need to do to be worthy to meet God?

What do we need to do to be worthy to mirror God's beauty?

How can we rejoice in the gladness of our heart?

How can I apply this in my life today?

QUESTIONS

What happens if we divest ourselves of God's beauteous robe
and forfeit our portion from His wondrous fountain?
What are God's beauteous robe and wondrous fountain
How can I apply this in my life today?

QUESTIONS

Why should we walk in God's statutes?

What should we do for God's pleasure?

How can we walk in God's statutes today?

How can I apply this in my life today?

QUESTIONS

Why should we not neglect God's commandments?

How do we attain God's good pleasure?

What does it mean to be addressed as Son of Man?

How can I apply this in my life today?

QUESTIONS

Where do we find rest?

How do we exhibit humbleness before God's face?

How can I apply this in my life today?

QUESTIONS

What happens when we magnify the cause of God?

What does it mean to have God shine upon us "with the light of eternity?"

How can I apply this in my life today?

QUESTIONS

How can we have God visit us?

How do we obtain the victory?

What is the victory?

How can I apply this in my life today?

QUESTIONS

What happens when we make mention of God while we are alive in this world?

What happens when God remembers us?

What does it mean to have our eyes solaced?

How can I apply this in my life today?

QUESTIONS

What are our sight and our hearing?

What happens when we testify unto God's exalted sanctity?

How can we hear with God's hearing or see with His sight to-day?

How can I apply this in my life today?

QUESTIONS

What should we be content with and thankful for?

What awaits a martyr in God's path?

What is a living martyr?

How can I apply this in my life today?

QUESTIONS

What are we supposed to do?

What happens if we become a martyr in god's path?

What does it mean to be a martyr?

How can I apply this in my life today?

QUESTIONS

What are we asked to strive toward?

What is greater than the creation of the universe?

Who are we?

What does it mean to tinge thy hair with blood?

How can I apply this in my life today?

QUESTIONS

What is the sign of love?

What does for everything there is a sign mean?

How can I apply this in my life today?

QUESTIONS

What does the rebel yearn for?

What does the sinful yearn for?

What does it mean to yearn for tribulation?

How can I apply this in my life today?

QUESTIONS

When should we walk in a way that demonstrates contentment with God's pleasure?

If we do not have trials in our longing to meet God, what will we have trouble attaining?

How can I apply this in my life today?

QUESTIONS

What is light and mercy?

What are we to hasten toward?

How can a calamity be God's providence?

How can I apply this in my life today?

QUESTIONS

What will pass?

How should we behave when we are prosperous?

How should we behave when we are abased?

How can we be abased?

How can I apply this in my life today?

QUESTIONS

Why should we not fear abasement?

What follows poverty?

What is the Lord of wealth?

How can I apply this in my life today?

QUESTIONS

If we want eternal dominion and everlasting life, what do we need to do?

How long does sovereignty last?

What can we do to forsake this mortal and fleeting sovereignty?

How can I apply this in my life today?

QUESTIONS

How are the servants of God tested?

How does fire test gold?

What does it mean to not busy ourselves with this world when we are to make this world a better place?

How can I apply this in my life today?

QUESTIONS

What does God wish for us?

What does God see as wealth?

What does it mean to be sanctified from possessions?

How can I apply this in my life today?

QUESTIONS

Whose wealth are we to bestow upon the poor?

What is more glorious than bestowing wealth on the poor?

What happens when we bestow wealth on the poor?

What does it mean to offer up our soul?

How can I apply this in my life today?

QUESTIONS

Where is God to be established?

What are we to do with the temple of being?

What is the temple of being and how do we cleanse it?

How can I apply this in my life today?

QUESTIONS

Where is God's home?

Where is God's place of revelation?

What are we supposed to do to God's home and the place of His revelation?

How do we sanctify our heart and cleanse our spirit?

How can I apply this in my life today?

Questions

When God rises above us, how does He appear?

What does it mean to put our hand into God's bosom?

How can I apply this in my life today?

QUESTIONS

How do we attain the joy of reunion with God?

What is the peerless wine?

How do we ascend unto God's heaven?

How can I apply this in my life today?

QUESTIONS

What have we busied ourselves with?

What do we miss as we slumber?

What do we need to do to have the Sun shine upon us?

How can I apply this in my life today?

QUESTIONS

What do we need to do to be fit for everlasting life and be worthy to meet God?

What has shone on us and breathed on us?

What does it mean that death, weariness, and trouble will not come upon us?

How can I apply this in my life today?

QUESTIONS

What is to be our garment?

Who created it for us?

How can we be the revelation of God's everlasting being?

How do we clothe ourselves in God's work (His creation and His Unity)?

How can I apply this in my life today?

QUESTIONS

What is God's gift to us?

What is it that none shall understand or anyone recount?

Why is God's majesty a gift?

Why is God's grandeur a token of His mercy to us?

How can I apply this in my life today?

QUESTIONS

What shall perturb souls?

What will we be hindered from doing? Why?

What does it mean to be a child of the Divine and Invisible Essence?

How can I apply this in my life today?

QUESTIONS

How much has God told us?

Has God told us all that is?

Why has God not told us all that he knows?

How can I apply this in my life today?

QUESTIONS

Why did God create all of us from the same dust?

What do we need to keep thinking about?

How should we be?

What signs should we make manifest?

How can I apply this in my life today?

QUESTIONS

What has God put within us?

Who are we to guard them from?

What does it mean to be a Treasury?

How is a Treasury guarded and how do we do that for ourselves?

How can I apply this in my life today?

QUESTIONS

What has God done for us?

What are we to do?

How are we to be content with God's pleasure?

How can I apply this in my life today?

QUESTIONS

What are we to write?

What is the ink of light?

What is the ink of the essence of our heart?

What is the crimson ink?

How can I apply this in my life today?

THE HIDDEN WORDS OF BAHÁ'U'LLÁH

Part II – from the Persian

PERSIAN HIDDEN WORDS #1

QUESTIONS

Where are we to abide?

Where are we to dwell to attain our goal?

What wings will take us to the realm of the infinite?

What do we do to live on the mount of faithfulness?

How can I apply this in my life today?

Questions

How is man different from the bird or the nightingale?

For a mere cupful, what have we turned away from?

What does it mean to be content with transient dust?

How can I apply this in my life today?

QUESTIONS

What are we to hold tight to?

What are we to plant in our hearts?

Whose companionship are we to treasure?

How can I apply this in my life today?

QUESTIONS

Where does a lover go and where does he find rest?

What is life and death to a true lover?

What would the true lover forsake to go to the beloved?

Why does this section start with O Son of Justice?

How can I apply this in my life today?

QUESTIONS

What is the most negligent thing men can do?

What is our adorning?

What should not be our adorning?

How can I apply this in my life today?

Persian Hidden Words #6

QUESTIONS

What will keep us from attaining God's everlasting dominion?

How big a remnant of envy will keep us from God?

What is God's kingdom of sanctity?

How can I apply this in my life today?

QUESTIONS

What are we very close to?

What do we need to do to advance into the immortal realm and enter the pavilion of eternity?

What do we need to give ear to?

How can I apply this in my life today?

QUESTIONS

What path must we be swift on?
What must we cleanse our heart with?
Where does the path of holiness lead?
What is involved with being on the path of holiness?
What is the burnish of the spirit?
How can I apply this in my life today?

PERSIAN HIDDEN WORDS #9

QUESTIONS

How does God address us?

How are doubt and certainty described?

What do we need to do to behold the veilless beauty?

How can I apply this in my life today?

QUESTIONS

What cannot recognize the Divine?

What does a mortal seek and take pleasure in?

How does the salutation O Son of Desire relate to this Hidden Word?

How can I apply this in my life today?

QUESTIONS

What do we need to do to perceive God's attributes?

What happens when we do those things?

What happens when we have a clear vision?

How can I apply this in my life today?

QUESTIONS

Man has two visions; what does each see?

What are we to close our eye to?

What are we to open one to?

How do we close one eye to the world?

How can I apply this in my life today?

QUESTIONS

What keeps us from sinking into utter loss?
What happens if we never see the beauty of the rose?
What does it mean to return to water and clay?
How can I apply this in my life today?

QUESTIONS

What are we not to abandon?
What are we not to set our affections on?
How does it feel to be referred to by God as O Friends?
How can I apply this in my life today?

QUESTIONS

What time is coming?

What will we miss when the nightingale of holiness stops unfolding the inner mysteries?

How can I apply this in my life today?

QUESTIONS

How does God address us?

How many speeches and how many melodies are revealed?

Who is hearing and understanding this?

How do we understand with our heart?

How can I apply this in my life today?

QUESTIONS

How do the gates to the Placeless stand?

How many have entered the celestial city?

How many have a pure heart and sanctified spirit?

How do we purify our heart and sanctify our spirit?

How can I apply this in my life today?

QUESTIONS

What are we to proclaim?

What station are we to strive towards?

What are we to learn and unravel?

How can I apply this in my life today?

QUESTIONS

Whose will are we to prefer?

What are we to desire?

How should our hearts be when we approach God?

How do we prefer God's will and desire what He desires for us?

How can I apply this in my life today?

QUESTIONS

How does God describe us?

How do we walk on the earth?

How do we reverse the picture of man described here in our own life?

How can I apply this in my life today?

QUESTIONS

What has felled our tree of hope?
Where is God and where are we?
Have we lost our chance to change this?
How can God be near us and we be far from Him?
How can I apply this in my life today?

QUESTIONS

How do we differ from the learned and the wise?

What have we done to ourselves with the veil of self?

If we have eyes, what are we to do?

What does it mean in this section to wonder?

How can I apply this in my life today?

QUESTIONS

How does God describe the plight of the celestial Youth?

Who bewails and laments?

What are we doing and how are we described?

How can I apply this in my life today?

QUESTIONS

How are we addressed in this Hidden Word?

How do our outward and inward selves differ?

Where are we leading people?

What actions in our lives does this describe and how can we change them?

How can I apply this in my life today?

QUESTIONS

What is bitter water like?

Where do the sunbeams fall?

How are we like bitter water?

How can I apply this in my life today?

QUESTIONS

Can friend and foe abide in one heart?

What is meant by our heart?

What are we to do with the stranger?

What does it mean to be friend in word?

How can I apply this in my life today?

QUESTIONS

What is meant by the human heart?

What have we done with our hearts?

What has God ordained for us?

How can I apply this in my life today?

QUESTIONS

How has God often found us?

What were we busied with?

What did God do when he found us?

How can I apply this in my life today?

QUESTIONS

What has God ordained for our training?

What did God provide for us before we were born?

What is God's purpose in caring for us?

How did we behave after God provided all this for us?

How can I apply this in my life today?

QUESTIONS

How does God address us?

What wafts over us?

How were we found?

How can I apply this in my life today?

QUESTIONS

What do we need to do to seek God?

How do we gaze upon God's beauty?

What cannot dwell together in our heart?

How can we close our eyes to the world today so that we may gaze upon God?

How can I apply this in my life today?

QUESTIONS

What did the hand of God's power do?

What can the contrary winds of self and passion do?

What is the healer of all our ills?

What are we to do with God's love?

How can I apply this in my life today?

QUESTIONS

What should we listen for?

Where should we sow the seeds of God's divine wisdom?

What should we water those seeds with?

If we do those things, what will happen?

How can I apply this in my life today?

QUESTIONS

What has God planted within the holy garden of paradise?

What are we to do now that the time for the tree to bear fruit has come?

What is the holy garden of paradise?

What are the flames of desire and passion?

How can I apply this in my life today?

QUESTIONS

What are we to kindle within our hearts?

What will soon be the only things accepted?

What must we quench?

How can I apply this in my life today?

Questions

When should the wise speak?

When should we offer our cup?

When should we cry out?

What are speaking, offering a cup, and crying out referring to?

How can I apply this in my life today?

QUESTIONS

What should we not cast away?

How would we cast it away?

From whence does the "river of everlasting life" flow?

How can I apply this in my life today?

QUESTIONS

What should we do with our cage?

Where should we soar?

Where should we abide?

How can we reside there?

How can I apply this in my life today?

QUESTIONS

What are we warned about trading?

How is our mortal world described?

What is the difference between the ease of a passing day and everlasting rest?

How can I apply this in my life today?

QUESTIONS

What are we to free ourselves from?

Can we always seize our chance?

What are some of the fetters of this world?

How can I apply this in my life today?

QUESTIONS

How would we feel if we saw immortal sovereignty?

What is our world?

Why does this Hidden Word refer to us as Son of My Hand-maid?

How can I apply this in my life today?

QUESTIONS

What do we need to do to enter the divine court of holiness?
What malice and envy do we need to purge from our heart?
How can I apply this in my life today?

QUESTIONS

How are we supposed to walk?

What is God's pleasure?

What are the four things we are instructed not to do?

What does it mean not to prefer our will over our friend's?

How can I apply this in my life today?

QUESTIONS

What should we not do?

Why should we not do those things?

How should we live?

What happens if we live that way?

How can I apply this in my life today?

Questions

What do we call truth?

What have we cast to the wind?

How do we not do all the things referred to in this Hidden Word?

How can I apply this in my life today?

QUESTIONS

What keeps us remote from the holy presence of the Loved One?

What are we deprived of?

What are the sweet savors of holiness, and what does it mean that they are breathing?

How can I apply this in my life today?

QUESTIONS

Of what are we the children?

Of what attire should we divest ourselves?

How can I apply this in my life today?

QUESTIONS

What should we not be proud of and what should we not be
ashamed of?

How should we treat each other?

What does it mean to be created from dust and returned to
dust?

How can I apply this in my life today?

QUESTIONS

What attributes of God are we urged to adorn ourselves with?

What should we tell the rich?

Who are the rich?

How can I apply this in my life today?

QUESTIONS

What should we put away and why?

What should we seek and why?

How can I apply this in my life today?

QUESTIONS

How should we react to wealth or poverty?
What is a wondrous gift?
How can I apply this in my life today?

QUESTIONS

Who has entered My house and who has been cast out?
Why has He suffered countless afflictions?
What do worldly friends do?
How can I apply this in my life today?

QUESTIONS

What is a barrier between the lover and his beloved?
Who shall illuminate the dwellers of heaven even as the sun en-
lightens the people of the earth?
Who shall enter the city of content and resignation?
How can I apply this in my life today?

QUESTIONS

Who are the poor?
What should we not focus on?
Who are we?
How can I apply this in my life today?

QUESTIONS

From where do we quaff the wine of immortal life?
What are we to cleanse ourselves from?
Do riches defile us? Why or why not?
How can I apply this in my life today?

QUESTIONS

What increases our sorrow?
What cleans the rust from our hearts?
What do we need to do to commune with God?
How can I apply this in my life today?

QUESTIONS

What does fellowship with the ungodly do to us?
What are we to beware of?
What is the God-created state of our hearts?
Who are the ungodly that we can easily walk with?
How can I apply this in my life today?

QUESTIONS

What can happen when we enter into fellowship with the righteous?

What have the righteous done?

What do the righteous and the true morn do?

How can I apply this in my life today?

QUESTIONS

What is engraved in clear characters?
Who can see those clear characters?
This Hidden Word refers to us as O Heedless Ones. What are we heedless of?
How can I apply this in my life today?

QUESTIONS

What is one of God's graces to us?
What is open to God?
How clear is what is in our heart to God?
How can I apply this in my life today?

QUESTIONS

What has God shed upon us?
What have we turned to?
What is the result of being content with the mortal cup?
How can I apply this in my life today?

QUESTIONS

What happens if we take the divine chalice of immortal life?
Who are we?
What does it mean to be of low aim?
How can I apply this in my life today?

QUESTIONS

What had God done with all our doings?
What is not effaced from God's sight?
What does it mean to be peoples of the world?
How can I apply this in my life today?

QUESTIONS

What are we to withdraw our hands from?

What has God pledged?

What does it mean to be an oppressor of the earth?

How can I apply this in my life today?

QUESTIONS

What can lead us into perilous ways and destruction?
Who are we?
What is the fiery charger of passion?
How can I apply this in my life today?

QUESTIONS

What is our tongue to be used for?
What are we to do when the fire of self overcomes us?
What does it mean that we are emigrants?
How can I apply this in my life today?

QUESTIONS

What will be laid bare and manifest before all people?

What does "Children of Fancy" mean?

What does it mean that the radiant dawn breaks above the horizon of eternal holiness?

How can I apply this in my life today?

QUESTIONS

Where are we in comparison to our desire?
What is God telling us about how we should approach him?
What do we need to do to approach God and enter His realm?
How can I apply this in my life today?

QUESTIONS

What ascends to heaven?
What do we need to cleanse our deeds from?
What will be accepted in the presence of the Adored One?
How can I apply this in my life today?

QUESTIONS

How does the realm of being compare to the domain of eternity?

What is it like to drink from the mystic chalice from the hands of the celestial Youth?

How do we pass beyond the world of mortality?

How can I apply this in my life today?

QUESTIONS

What has effaced our faithfulness to the covenant?

What did God do when he saw that we have not kept the covenant?

What does it mean to enter into a covenant with God?

How can I apply this in my life today?

QUESTIONS

What does God liken us to?
Where does He say we are?
What are we to do and why are we to do it?
What is a finely tempered sword and how are we like one?
How can I apply this in my life today?

QUESTIONS

How does God describe us?

What are we warned about?

How will we emerge if we rend asunder our veil of heedlessness?

How do we rend asunder our veil of heedlessness?

How can I apply this in my life today?

QUESTIONS

What have we abandoned?

Why have we abandoned it?

How do we avoid being gathered under the one-coloured covering of dust?

How can I apply this in my life today?

QUESTIONS

What are we not to set our affections on?
What are we like?
What are we to take heed of?
How can I apply this in my life today?

QUESTIONS

How is guidance now given and how is it different than in the past?

What must we all do to distinguish ourselves?

What is the difference between words and deeds?

How can I apply this in my life today?

QUESTIONS

What was not found from the dwellers of earth?
What does this say about mankind's capability and capacity?
How can I apply this in my life today?

QUESTIONS

What are we to sow in our hearts?
How must the soil of our hearts be?
What must we water the seeds with?
What will the seeds produce if we care for them?
How can I apply this in my life today?

QUESTIONS

What are our wings for?

What do we use them for more often?

What does it mean that he gave us a comb to dress His raven locks?

How can I apply this in my life today?

QUESTIONS

Why must we give forth goodly and wondrous fruits?
What is the secret of wealth?
What do results depend upon?
What is all-sufficient to us?
What results might this be referring to?
How can I apply this in my life today?

QUESTIONS

Who are the basest of all men?
How does God describe those who yield no fruit?
What does it mean to yield no fruit?
How can I apply this in my life today?

QUESTIONS

Who are we to spend our money on?
Who are the best of men?
Why should we spend our money?
How can I apply this in my life today?

QUESTIONS

What is the first sentence is referring to?

God offers us a challenge in the third sentence. How will we respond to the challenge?

How can I apply this in my life today?

ABOUT THE AUTHOR

Jan Perry is a Baha'i taking baby-steps to use the Hidden Words as a guide to living.

Made in United States
Troutdale, OR
04/23/2025

30846499R00096